Buns!

and

The Big Dig

By Jenny Jinks

Illustrated by
Daniel Limon

The Letter S

Trace the lower and upper case letter with a finger. Sound out the letter.

*Around,
around*

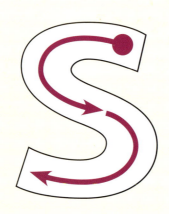

*Around,
around*

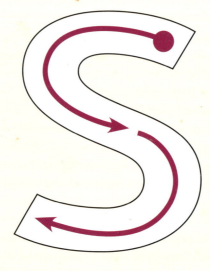

4

Some words to familiarise:

Matt   bun   Sniff

High-frequency words:

has   a   no   go   to

of   you   is   in

Tips for Reading 'Buns!'

- Practise the words listed above before reading the story.

- If the reader struggles with any of the other words, ask them to look for sounds they know in the word. Encourage them to sound out the words and help them read the words if necessary.

- After reading the story, ask the reader why Sniff got a big tum

Fun Activity

Draw and decorate a bun!

Buns!

Matt has a bun.

Sam has a hot bun.

Ben has a pink bun.

Lin has a big bun.

Mel has lots of buns.

Yum, yum!

No buns for
you, Sniff.

Sniff gets lots of buns.

Sniff has a big tum.

The Letter D

Trace the lower and upper case letter with a finger. Sound out the letter.

*Around,
up,
down*

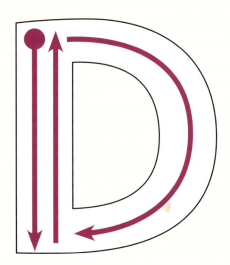

*Down,
up,
around*

Some words to familiarise:

stick   rock   sand

High-frequency words:

is   on   a   as   no   he
up   in   the

Tips for Reading 'The Big Dig'

- Practise the words listed above before reading the story.

- If the reader struggles with any of the other words, ask them to look for sounds they know in the word. Encourage them to sound out the words and help them read the words if necessary.

- After reading the story, ask the reader what Sniff found.

Fun Activity

Discuss what other things you can dig up!

The Big Dig

Matt is on a big dig.

Sniff is as well.

No, Sniff!

21

Matt digs. He digs up a stick.

Matt digs and digs.
He digs up a rock.

Sniff gets in.

She digs and digs and digs.

Matt is in the sand.

Sniff digs up Matt.

But Sniff will not stop.
Dig, dig, dig.

Book Bands for Guided Reading

The Institute of Education book banding system is a scale of colours that reflects the various levels of reading difficulty. The bands are assigned by taking into account the content, the language style, the layout and phonics. Word, phrase and sentence level work is also taken into consideration.

Maverick Early Readers are a bright, attractive range of books covering the pink to white bands. All of these books have been book banded for guided reading to the industry standard and edited by a leading educational consultant.

Pink
Red
Yellow
Blue
Green
Orange
Turquoise
Purple
Gold
White

To view the whole Maverick Readers scheme, visit our website at
www.maverickearlyreaders.com

Or scan the QR code above to view our scheme instantly!